Success Cycles
and Secrets

■ ■ ■

Power Twins

By Prince Handley

University of Excellence Press

Copyright © 2009 by Prince Handley
All Rights Reserved.

UNIVERSITY OF EXCELLENCE PRESS
Los Angeles ■ London ■ Tel Aviv

ISBN-13: 978-0692272749
ISBN-10: 0692272747

Printed in the U.S.A.

First Edition

The only book you need on Success Cycles

TABLE OF CONTENTS

FOREWORD

The reader is guaranteed *continued* **vision and** *cycles* **of success** from the principles in this book.

You will be fruitful if you do what you learn in this book. It is great to be successful in your life or profession ... but what about **continuous cycles of success.**

And ... what about **fresh revelation and organic vision to dumbfound your enemies and bless those around you** ... including those in need?

I'm talking about creativity that wakes you up at night. You not only need to—but you will want to— **color outside the lines**.

Do what this book teaches you and **you will find yourself continuously "ahead of the curve."** But, let me warn you, you won't fit the mold of a normal person.

There are eight power twins for success cycles and continued—*organic*—vision. **You will learn them all**. Don't be satisfied with just one success ... make it continuous!

Situations vary in life; you may not always come up against situations that have been codified. But this book will teach you principles you can transfer into every arena of life.

Go BIG or stay at home. It's time to wind your clock for maximum destiny. Everything—and everyone—is prepared and waiting on YOU. **Can you hear God?!**

Success Cycles
and Secrets

■ ■ ■

Power Twins

No matter how successful we become in life, it will not be of any time value unless we know God personally. If we know God through His Son, Jesus the Messiah, then we have eternal life. [John 3:16]

One measure of our success in life is how many of our associates—or destiny partners—will make it to Heaven. If we have children, one measure of our success in life is how many of our children make it to Heaven.

5

If we know the Lord, we are living part of our eternal life NOW, while here on earth, and then in Heaven. It will never end. Jesus taught us:

"What does it profit a man if he gains all the world, and loses his own soul? Also, what shall a man give in exchange, or to buy back, his soul?" [Mark 8:36 - Matthew 16:26]

We need to have TOTAL success in life: in this life on earth and in the eternal beyond; and God has provided just such means to attain that goal. God has given us EVERYTHING WE NEED for:

LIFE, and

GODLINESS.

"According as His divine power has given unto us ALL THINGS that pertain unto life and godliness, through the knowledge of Him that has called us to glory and virtue." [2 Peter 1:3]

He has given us PROMISES so that we can share or partner with Him in His divine expansion--or growth of descendants--after we have escaped, by His saving grace, the ruin that is in the world through lust. In other words, after we are born again and start serving Christ, **we can partner and be a companion with God** in successfully bearing fruit: that is, growing other seed-descendants. **These include our own children** who are born again while also reaching out to the rest of the world.

"Whereby are given to us exceeding great and precious promises: that by these you might be partakers of the divine nature, having escaped the corruption that is in the world through lust." [2 Peter 1:4]

We should **BELIEVE** this and **EXPECT** it. **Your children should be your greatest successes.** If not, something is wrong, or out of place.

I guarantee you success cycles and continued vision! **You will not be barren or unfruitful, if you practice what I am about to teach you.** Also, **you will have an abundant entrance into Heaven**. Remember, there are rewards in Heaven for your labor of love and faithfulness here on earth.

Jesus wants to be able to say to you when you enter Heaven: *"Well done, you good and faithful servant. You have been faithful over a few things; I will make you ruler over many things. Enter into the joy of the Lord."* [Matthew 25:21]

You need continued vision for vitality. The Bible says, *"Without a vision, the people perish."* [Proverb 29:18] To be successful in this life and to prepare for life in Heaven--and to maintain continued vision so we will be fresh and vibrant--there are eight TWIN STRATEGIES to help you.

The FIRST TWO POWER TWINS for success cycles and continued--*organic*--vision are as follows:

Enthusiastic Desire PLUS Faith; and,

Decisive Nature PLUS Virtue.

7

We will now discuss these first two twins. Remaining twins for success cycles and continued--*organic*--vision will be discussed in later sections of the book.

◻ ENTHUSIASTIC DESIRE PLUS FAITH

If you do not have burning desires and goals throughout life, you will become bored. The English word **"enthusiasm" means "intense enjoyment or interest."** It has **its root in the Greek word 'enthous,' meaning possessed by God**.

Josiah became king of Judah when he was eight years old and reigned for 31 years. *"And like unto him was there no king before him, that turned to the Lord with ALL HIS HEART, and with all his soul, and with all his might, according to all the law of Moses; neither after him arose there any like unto him."* [2 Kings 23:25]

There is a wonderful promise in Mark 11:24 which Jesus declared: *"Therefore I say unto you, Whatever things you DESIRE, when you pray, believe that you receive them, and you shall have them."*

Another wonderful promise in Psalm 37:4 states: *"Delight yourself in the Lord, and He shall give you the DESIRES of your heart."*

When you have pleasurable emotion in the Lord, when you delight in Him--**when you are ENTHUSED in your worship of Him--then He will give you the DESIRES of your heart**. He first gives them to you **by placing** them in your heart and mind. And secondly, He gives them to you **by granting** them--bringing them to fruition after you have consistently applied your FAITH.

8

These desires will many times be to do GREAT THINGS; and the enemy, the devil, will lie to you and tell you that you can NOT accomplish them. But the devil is a liar and God is truth. This is one way **you know** that **those desires in your heart to do BIG THINGS for Christ are from God**: because the devil is trying to talk you out of them!

When you **combine your good desires with faith** . . . ENTHUSIASTIC DESIRE PLUS FAITH . . . you have **an unbeatable combination**. You can begin to **PLAN your future prayerfully based upon the God given desires of your heart**.

That's one reason it is important to read and meditate upon the Word of God daily so you will KNOW and develop the will of God for your life.

Remember, **you can CREATE with your faith**. Hebrews 11:1 tell us, *"Now faith is the substance of things hoped for, the evidence of things not seen."* **Faith is the underpinning** or support--a title deed (as in property)--that lets you KNOW you have the objects or affairs you do not yet see.

It is a wonderful thing to have FAITH, but if you have a PLAN incorporating your desires to go along with your faith, it is even better! Here's a SECRET that will allow you to SEE many MIRACLES:

If your PLANS fit into God's plans ...

you will have God's FAITH ...

and God's faith ALWAYS WORKS!

⬛ DECISIVE NATURE PLUS VIRTUE

You need to be able to **make decisions based upon knowledge and quality input.** Once again, this is where it is important to read and meditate upon the Word of God daily. You need DIRECTION in the many matters of life that face you now . . . and also about future planning. God has given us everything we need for LIFE and GODLINESS through His PROMISES and the KNOWLEDGE of Christ.

In business we need to draw upon quality research, marketing, and experience (sometimes the input of others). And we need to KNOW when to act. **Timing is a KEY to success** in many courses of action. Bill Gates, founder of Microsoft, says that when he knows that something is right, and that the timing is right, he goes into it with MASSIVE ACTION. However, **without VIRTUE a decision can have disastrous effects eternally and with no substance temporally** here on earth.

The Greek word for VIRTUE in the New testament is arete: it means excellence and valor. It also includes the connotation of the miracles. We need to be people of EXCELLENCE. Our nature should be to make excellent DECISIONS based upon VIRTUE.

"And whatever you do, do it heartily, as to the Lord, and not unto men. Knowing that of the Lord you shall receive the reward of the inheritance; for you serve the Lord Christ." [Colossians 3:23-24]

Make your decisions based upon the fact that God is watching you!

There are several words for TIME in the Bible, but **in our discussion here of DECISIVE NATURE we are talking about a due season of time**, or **an opportune season of time**. It is the meaning which if you **miss the window** of time presented you--or available at this particular time--then you will **MISS the opportunity!** In the New Testament it is the Greek word "kairos."

An example of exercising a DECISIVE NATURE along with VIRTUE is in the Old Testament in the *Book of Esther* when the Jews were facing extermination in 127 provinces from India to Ethiopia. Mordecai told Queen Esther:

"For if you altogether hold your peace at this time, then shall there enlargement and deliverance arise to the Jews from another place; but you and your father's house shall be destroyed: and who knows whether you have come to the kingdom for such a time as this?"

Ruth is another example of a person who exercised a DECISIVE NATURE and VIRTUE when she decided to go to Israel with her mother-in-law. She said: *"Entreat me not to leave you, or to return from following after you: for where you go, I will go; and where you lodge, I will lodge. Your people shall be my people, and your God will be my God."* [Ruth 1:16]

➡ **Rest for creativity, development, and new ideas**.

➡ **It's alright to be eccentric in the eyes of society**.

I guarantee you success and continued vision! You will not be barren or unfruitful, if you practice what I am teaching you in this book. Also, you will have an abundant entrance into Heaven. Remember, there are rewards in Heaven for your labor of love and faithfulness here on earth.

Jesus wants to say to you when you enter Heaven: *"Well done, you good and faithful servant. You have been faithful over a few things; I will make you ruler over many things. Enter into the joy of the Lord."* [Matthew 25:21]

You need continued vision for vitality. The Bible says, *"Without a vision, the people perish."* [Proverb 29:18] To be successful in this life and to prepare for life in Heaven ... and to maintain continued vision so we will be fresh and vibrant ... there are eight (8) TWIN STRATEGIES to help you.

Previously we discussed the FIRST TWO TWINS for success cycles and continued--*organic*--vision:

Enthusiastic Desire PLUS Faith; and,

Decisive Nature PLUS Virtue.

Now, we will discuss the next two twins. They are as follows:

Specialized Knowledge PLUS Spiritual Knowledge; and,

Quest for Excellence PLUS Temperance.

The remaining twins for success cycles and continued vision will be discussed in later sections of this book.

▣ SPECIALIZED KNOWLEDGE PLUS SPIRITUAL KNOWLEDGE

If you are going to be used greatly by God, then you will have to make up your mind ahead of time that you are willing to do things--*and exploits*--that are out of the ordinary. Jesus did not fit into the normal mold of man, even though He was God in human flesh. He was a perfect man ... but he was focused on doing the will of God ... not the will of man.

Likewise, if you make the decision to do the will of God during your time here on earth, then neither will you will fit into the normal mold of man: **you will seem eccentric to the world. You will find yourself continuously "ahead of the curve."** The definition of eccentric is as follows:

Unconventional and slightly strange;

Not placed centrally or having its axis placed centrally.

But you see, this definition is from the perspective of what is "normal" and **God did NOT call us to be normal by the world's standards**. Rather, the normal Christian life is abnormal to the world.

The origin of the word "eccentric" is from the Greek **"ekkentros"**: "ek" meaning "out of" plus "kentron" meaning "center" or **"out of center."**

John Steward Mill gives an insightful comment of truth concerning this:

*"Eccentricity has always abounded when and where strength of character has abounded; and **the amount of eccentricity in society has always been proportioned to the amount of genius, mental vigor and moral courage which it contained.** That so few men now dare to be eccentric marks the chief danger of our time."*

➡ **Color outside the lines**

Specialized knowledge is highly dependent upon genius and mental vigor.

The second of these two, **mental vigor, can complement what may be lacking in the first of the two: genius**.

What is that GREAT THING you want to do for God? Do you have the SPECIALIZED KNOWLEDGE to attain that goal? Are you willing to sacrifice, study, and research to obtain the knowledge required to complete the task? Don't be a lazy Christian. **God called us to excellence, not complacency!**

I have been on this planet for several scores of years, and I still spend much time studying and researching to find NEW, BETTER, and MORE PRODUCTIVE ways to reach the world for Christ and to help my fellow man.

Don't be afraid—and never get too old—to go back to school for more formal education.

One of the best schools to learn **Entertainment, Media and the Arts**, and one which I fully endorse, is *Full Sail University* based in Winter Park, Florida, USA. They may be contacted by phone at 800.226.7625. You may contact them on the web at www.fullsail.edu. **Some** of their major fields of study are:

- Film Production;

- Recording Arts;

- Computer Animation;

- Digital Arts and Media;

- Entertainment Business;

- Sports Marketing and Media;

- Show Production and Touring;

- Game Design and Development;

- Emerging Technology & Systems Engineering.

You can tell them that Prince Handley recommended you.

We are living in a day like the prophet Daniel described where *"knowledge shall be increased"* and we should take advantage of it to advance the kingdom of God. Daniel, in a passage of scripture dealing with the end

15

times, tells us "*... but the people that do know their God shall be strong, and do exploits.*" [Daniel 11:32] **Exploit**, in the sense used here, **means** literally **"to do successively unfolding bold, courageous works!"**

There are many other ways to influence society and to reach the world for Christ other than through the media. And there are many NEW ways to help yourself gain SUCCESS! **Pray and ask God to reveal these to you.** Then, obey Him and be diligent to study in order to prepare yourself to be used by the Master: to be a good steward.

No amount of SPECIALIZED KNOWLEDGE, however, will be of significant time value without SPIRITUAL KNOWLEDGE. No matter how successful we become in life, it will not be of any time value unless we know God personally. If we know God through His Son, Jesus the Messiah, then we have eternal life. [John 3:16]

One of the measures of a person's success in life is how many of their children make it to Heaven. If we know the Lord, we are living part of our eternal life NOW, while here on earth, and then in Heaven. It will never end!

Jesus taught us, *"What does it profit a man if he gains all the world, and loses his own soul? Also, what shall a man give in exchange, or to buy back, his soul?"* [Mark 8:36 - Matthew 16:26]

We need to have TOTAL success in life: in this life on earth and in the eternal beyond; and God has provided

16

just such means to attain that goal. **God has given us everything we need for:**

LIFE, and

GODLINESS.

"According as His divine power has given unto us ALL THINGS that pertain unto life and godliness, through the knowledge of Him that has called us to glory and virtue." [2 Peter 1:3]

He has given us PROMISES so that we can share or partner with Him in His divine expansion--or growth of descendants--after we have escaped, by His saving grace, the ruin that is in the world through lust. In other words, after we are born again and start serving Christ, **we can partner** and be a companion **with God** in successfully bearing fruit: that is, growing other seed-descendants. These include our own children who are born again while also reaching out to the rest of the world.

"Whereby are given to us exceeding great and precious promises: that by these you might be partakers of the divine nature, having escaped the corruption that is in the world through lust." [2 Peter 1:4]

We should BELIEVE this and EXPECT it. **Our children should be our greatest disciples**. If not, something is wrong, or out of place.

Learn the PROMISES in God's Word; believe them and appropriate them by faith. Take quality time daily to study and meditate in God's Word. I usually separate my "study time" from my "devotional time." In the morning, before I start my active day, I have my devotional time where I just want God to speak to me and minister to me through His Word, even before I have my prayer time. I made a rule years ago: **"No Bible, no breakfast."** Eat the Word of God first. Jesus said, *"It is written: Man shall not live by bread alone, but by every word that proceeds out of the mouth of God."* [Matthew 4:4 and Torah: Deuteronomy 8:3]

When you study the Bible, **ask the Holy Spirit to speak to you, and to teach you so you can teach others**. The scripture instructs us, *"Study to show yourself approved unto God, a workman that does not need to be ashamed, rightly dividing the word of truth."* [2 Timothy 2:15]

Combining SPECIALIZED KNOWLEDGE with SPIRITUAL KNOWLEDGE will provide you a powerful impetus for ongoing success and continued vision. **To be really successful we need to share our success with others**: our family, our brothers and sisters in Christ, our community, and the world.

THE MORE YOU KNOW . . . THE MORE THE HOLY SPIRIT CAN USE! This applies not only to mental knowledge but also knowledge gained through the acquisition of physical skills or craftsmanship. Bezaleel was such a man:

"And the Lord spoke unto Moses, saying, See, I have called by name Bezaleel the son of Uri, the son of Hur, of the tribe of Judah: and I have filled him with the Spirit of God, in wisdom, and in understanding, and in

knowledge, and in all manner of workmanship, to devise cunning works, to work in gold, and in silver, and in brass, and in cutting of stones, to set them, and in carving of timber, to work in all manner of workmanship." [Exodus 31:1-5]

When SPECIALIZED KNOWLEDGE is combined with SPIRITUAL KNOWLEDGE, there is a holy anointing upon our lives: our talents, skills, and abilities. Together, they not only complement each other, but they synergize each other. You will be a candidate for MIRACLES ... real miracles!

But always remember: ***"Knowledge puffs up, but love edifies."*** [1 Corinthians 8:1] **Temper your knowledge** (both specialized and spiritual) **with LOVE!**

Daniel was a leader, counselor, and basically Prime Minister in three different foreign kingdoms (in which he was captive) partly because of his knowledge base. The Bible tells us concerning Daniel and the three Hebrew teenagers who accompanied him into captivity:

"Children in whom was no blemish, but well favored, and skillful in all wisdom, and cunning in knowledge, and understanding science, and such as had ability ..." [Daniel 1:4]

⬛ QUEST FOR EXCELLENCE PLUS TEMPERANCE

The Bible tells us another of the secrets of Daniel's success:

"It pleased Darius to set over the kingdom a hundred and twenty princes, which should be over the whole

kingdom; and over these three presidents: of whom Daniel was first, so that the princes might give accounts unto the presidents, and the king should have no damage."

"Then this Daniel was preferred above the presidents and princes, because an EXCELLENT spirit was in him; and the king thought to set him over the whole realm." [Daniel 6:1-3]

The word here used for "excellent" is "yateer" and in its root form means "preeminent, or very exceedingly excellent." That's because the spirit that was in Daniel was the Holy Spirit. **Because of Daniel's separation and devotion to God, he manifested a quality of excellence in whatever he attempted**.

The Greek word for virtue in the New Testament is "arête": it means excellence and valor. We need to be people of EXCELLENCE. **Our nature should be to make excellent decisions based upon virtue**.

"And whatever you do, do it heartily, as to the Lord, and not unto men. Knowing that of the Lord you shall receive the reward of the inheritance; for you serve the Lord Christ." [Colossians 3:23-24]

Don't compare yourself with someone else; just do what you know God wants you to do. Do your best, don't be satisfied with low quality work or effort. It's interesting that the origin of the word mediocre is from the Latin "mediocris" which means of "middle height or degree" but literally means "somewhat rugged or mountainous." It is derived from the words "medius" for "middle" and "ocris" for "rugged mountain."

To do mediocre work is actually harder on you because you are causing your conscience to condemn you. It is like climbing a rugged mountain. The Bible says, *"For if our heart condemn us, God is greater than our heart, and knows all things."* [1 John 3:20] The EXCELLENT choice may be more of a sacrifice temporarily, but it will be easier on you in the long term. You will never go wrong striving for excellence!

Practice excellence in your CHARACTER. Be transparent and keep your word. Psalm 15 is a good start for practical living and developing excellence in character. Also, *"Loving our neighbor as we do ourselves, and doing unto him as we would have him do to us,"* is the guideline our Master set before us.

Practice excellence in your WORK. Be a good steward for your earthly employer **and** your Heavenly employer. Colossians 3:22 instructs us NOT to do sight-labor, that is: work that needs watching ... or working because someone is watching.

In your quest for excellence, develop your skills to the BEST of your ability. Be a good manager of what God has given you and over which God has placed you. **Keep improving and growing in your knowledge base, your acumen, and your skills**. Study the earlier part of this book to help develop excellence in acumen; study the section on "Decisive Nature and Virtue."

Along with the quest for excellence you need to partner with temperance, or self control. Many people, on their quest for excellence, do NOT allow for **rest or leisure**. This is **vital to VISION and CONTINUED SUCCESS**.

Rest, and also quietness, is necessary for wholeness. A key scripture and principle that I have tried to practice in my life for many years is found in Isaiah 30:15:

"For thus says the Lord God, the Holy One of Israel: In returning and rest shall you be saved; and in quietness and in confidence shall be your strength."

The word leisure comes from the Latin word "licere" which means "to be permitted." The Latin word for work is "negotium" which means "non-leisure." **Most so-called advanced societies today have turned this around** and view leisure as non-work!

Tim Hansel, in his book *When I Relax I Feel Guilty*, points out that the Greeks stressed the centrality of leisure, but they added another important facet. The Greek word for work was "ascholia," which means "absence of leisure." The word for leisure was "schole," which leads to the English words for school and scholarship. **Leisure, then, was a time for growth and development.**

➡ Leisure is more than just non-work. It is when we PERMIT ourselves time for rest, growth, and development. **Leisure is BOTH the embryo and the catalyst for creativity, and for NEW experiences, people, play, and places.**

We have to permit ourselves the time **to rest … to recreate … and to create!**

➡ **Be involved in propagating living development**

➡ **Share your success--and vision--with others**

Previously we discussed the FIRST FOUR TWINS for success cycles and continued--*organic*--vision:

Enthusiastic Desire PLUS Faith

Decisive Nature PLUS Virtue

Specialized Knowledge PLUS Spiritual Knowledge

Quest for Excellence PLUS Temperance

Now, we will discuss the fifth twin:

Organic Spiritual Endeavor PLUS Patience

The last three twins for repeated--*cycles*--of success and organic vision will be discussed later in the book.

■ ORGANIC SPIRITUAL ENDEAVOR PLUS PATIENCE

As we become successful we share our success with others: our family, our brothers and sisters in faith, our community, and the world. We need to have TOTAL success in life: in this life on earth and in the eternal beyond; and God has provided just such means to attain that goal. We discussed that **God has given us EVERYTHING WE NEED for:**

LIFE, and

GODLINESS.

"According as His divine power has given unto us ALL THINGS that pertain unto life and godliness, through the knowledge of Him that has called us to glory and virtue." [2 Peter 1:3]

He has given us PROMISES so that we can share or partner with Him in His divine expansion--or growth of descendants--after we have escaped, by His saving grace, the ruin that is in the world through lust. In other words, after we are born again and start serving Christ, we can partner and be a companion with God in successfully bearing fruit: that is, **growing other seed-descendants**. These include our own children who are born again while also reaching out to the rest of the world.

"Whereby are given to us exceeding great and precious promises: that by these you might be partakers of the divine nature, having escaped the corruption that is in the world through lust." [2 Peter 1:4]

Now ... **how do we use the precepts we have learned** in the previous sections of this book so as **to be involved in ORGANIC SPIRITUAL ENDEAVOR?** In other words, how can we involve ourselves in powerful, prolonged, and productive effort that will be self multiplying and profitable, not only temporally here on Planet Earth but also eternally in Heaven?

The answer: Be actively engaged in **organic growth** in some kind of service for the Lord! **Be involved in a work that is propagating living, continuous development of the Kingdom of God.**

The definition of the word propagate is **"to breed by natural (or supernatural) processes from a parent origin**; to promote an idea or knowledge widely; to transmit in a particular direction." My purpose in this section is to tell you the **specifics** of how to accomplish this.

COLOR OUTSIDE THE LINES

I know a man who is an industrialist. That is his calling from God: to start, build and manage industries. The **vision** God gave him to operate in **organic**---life giving continuing **success**---is to use the profits from his factories to go around the world holding MIRACLE meetings where people find Messiah Jesus as Savior. Multitudes are healed and lives changed through his success. Plus, he prospers exceedingly in industry.

There are around 60,000 people groups on Planet Earth, with Christians in most regions of the earth. With the expansion of global trade, internet access, and communications, many--if not most--of these groups understand and view themselves as one worldwide church in an interconnected world. **To be involved in Kingdom Work is to be involved with the heart and purpose of God**. It is to be involved **locally and globally** ... plus **temporally and eternally**.

The earth is getting smaller with regard to travel, communications, and interfacing of cultures. At the same time the church is becoming more inter-tribal. We see the horizon of the fulfillment of Jesus' prophecy that the Good News will be preached, proclaimed, or published before the time of His return.

"And the gospel must first be published [preached] among all nations." [Mark 13:10]

The word for nations here used is "ethnos"--as in ethnic group--meaning "a race of the same habit, or culture, or tribe."

Read and study the Biblical pattern of church growth in the Book of Acts. Certain things are evidentiary and **these same patterns are manifest in any POWER GROWTH church today.**

Notice this very obvious cycle of church or synagogue growth as outlined below. Then ask yourself this question: *"Is this what I see happening today?"*

1. When people believed in Jesus, and after they were baptized, a group was formed for:

    Worship;

    Teaching;

    Prayer;

    Helps; and,

    Evangelism.

2. Prophets and teachers were raised up by the Holy Spirit.

3. The Christians prayed and fasted.

4. The Holy Spirit called out apostles.

5. These apostles were sent out (NOT "released") by the believers after hands were laid on them.

6. As the apostles went to different areas they preached the Good News.

7. Other churches were raised up as a result of the preaching and the work of the apostles.

8. The churches grew and ministered to the believers, the community, and the world.

Notice, this is the NORMAL PATTERN of church growth. **This is to be expected today! It should be a regular practice** of a local church to SEND OUT workers: both for long term commitment and for short term service.

Notice, in Acts 13:1-4, it was the Holy Spirit who **CALLED** the apostles (verse 2) and it was the Holy Spirit who **SENT** them (verse 4). **In between the calling and the sending was the ratification by the elders with the laying on of hands** (verse 3). The apostles were NOT "released by men" **... it was the Holy Spirit who called and sent them**.

Note: If workers are "released" to ministry, that implies that they have (up to that point) been in bondage; which in many cases--*sad to say*--is probably true.

WARNING #1:

It is not enough just to see new churches being raised up. **This is where many POWER CHURCHES become deceived into complacency and become spiritually diffused**. There are two (2) main causes for this effect:

☞ They see many new churches being raised up, but begin to lack clarity or conciseness of mission or vision. **Over time they become spread out and increased in numbers but diffused in power**. Sometimes this is because of pride, or due to comparing themselves with other regional churches. Sometimes it is because of lack of sacrifice they **were** willing to render at the outset.

☞ They do NOT bring NEW POWERFUL LIFE **back into** their parent body.

This can be prevented and offset by **sending out short term mission groups** for a period of three to six weeks. These groups may go to a nearby region or they may go far away overseas to another country. They may combine evangelism, medical, and help ministries. They may go to un-evangelized territories, or they may go to assist those who have previously been sent out by the parent church; or they may go assist missionaries and Christian workers from other church groups.

This will result in a TRIPLE blessing:

> It will inject LIFE back into the parent church when they return from their short term ministry and share their testimonies;

> It will also inject LIFE into the area where they are sent; and,

> It will inject LIFE into the ones sent, influencing their future growth and service for the Lord.

WARNING #2:

It is of **great spiritual detriment** for the new churches, or individuals, being raised up to feel, or be instructed, that they are UNDER THE COVERING of the parent church.

> They may be accountable to the parent church, or other bodies, but **their covering is CHRIST AND HIS BLOOD ... NOT men or the church!** To teach otherwise is to cause them to lean on men and not the Lord, and to become

29

disciples of men and not Christ. This is one of Satan's tricks to quench TRUE evangelistic and prophetic ministry, and to lure them into a false sense of safety or covering.

 This teaching will usually be prevalent where potential candidates for ministry or the mission field are taught that they are not ready to be "released" from the parent body. **To be "released" is implying that they are being held in "bondage."** *"Who the Son sets FREE is free indeed ... absolutely!"* [John 8:36] They may not be ready to be sent out, but they surely should not be held in bondage, nor have that thought implied.

"Where the Spirit of the Lord is, there is liberty!" [2 Corinthians 3:17]

Be part of an organic church growth ... or organic ministry growth. Not indirectly ... but DIRECTLY. It is often said, *"If you can't go in person, then go by your prayers ... or go with your money."* Surely we can share by any of the three means: going, praying, and giving. But **be involved in ALL THREE**. Now, if you are elderly, or constrained in some way that you can't go yourself, the Lord understands. But be involved as much as you can: for your sake, for your church and ministry's sake, and for the sake of those to whom you could or should be ministering.

➡ **Pass "Go" and pick up $200. Take a power rest**.

If you are very busy in your business, ministry, or family life, **try to set aside vacation time to go on a**

30

ministry trip overseas or to some area in great need. If you are in a geographic area where there are no power churches or ministries, then pray for the Lord's direction. He may want you to START such a ministry. There are lots of good ministry groups who need help. You can contact them on the internet.

If you can, let your family be involved with you. Young children should not go to some areas because of sanitation, dehydration, and other risks. There is a great need in many countries for water and for wells to be drilled. There is a big need in many areas for other helps such as medical missions. **Whatever you do, combine it with preaching the Good News**. Some groups do lots of social work but never share the Gospel. Others do lots of evangelism but never help meet needs of the local people. **Do both!**

Be involved in ministry that is sending out the workers, birthing or planting new churches, preaching and teaching to facilitate the MIRACLE working power of God. You may be a business person that God has anointed to help reach the world for Christ; but minister personally, as well as through your business. **It will keep you creative, and help you to be even more successful while maintaining continued vision**. The anointing will keep you vibrant! Jesus sent out his followers -- and He is sending YOU out -- to:

- Preach and teach;

- Heal the sick;

- Cast out demons.

This threefold ministry, or triangulation of mission, will empower you and your ministry; it will keep you **FRESH under the anointing of the Spirit** so that you will SEE and EXPERIENCE MIRACLES: real miracles for the glory of God. **You will be continuously creative, causing you to be more successful and to have continued vision!** These things began Jesus both to DO and to TEACH ... and these things He would have us to DO and to TEACH! [Acts 1:1]

Most of the people reading this book are interested in being successful so that they may share their success. My advice to you is this: **"Go big or stay at home!"** In other words, don't make your life a hobby or an avocation. Your whole life should center around God's will for you. Or rather, your whole life should be in **the CENTER of God's will**. If not, start praying to that end.

We should always be willing to make changes for the Lord; that is part of discipleship. However; there are times we have to wait ... because God is developing things or situations where we are going to be sent ... or because He is developing things in our lives ... or both!

Patience is really cheerful, or hopeful, endurance. True biblical patience, as expressed by the Greek word "hupomone" is constancy. It is the kind of enduring patience, or patient continuance in well doing. **It is knowing the will of God for this season of your life, and looking forward to being used by God in SPECIAL SERVICE in the future, also!**

➡ What is your vision for using organic success

➡ Use your success to propagate help for others

So far we have discussed the FIRST FIVE TWINS for success cycles and continued--*organic*--vision:

Enthusiastic Desire PLUS Faith

Decisive Nature PLUS Virtue

Specialized Knowledge PLUS Spiritual Knowledge

Quest for Excellence PLUS Temperance

Organic Spiritual Endeavor PLUS Patience

In this part of the book we will cover the LAST THREE TWINS:

Principles of Value PLUS Godliness

Like-minded Associates PLUS Brotherly Kindness

Vehicle for Attainment PLUS Love

As you progress in your continued vision with organic success, **you will begin to develop patience ...** knowing that the Divine Plan is being worked out in and through your life. You will begin to identify and appreciate the destiny to which you have been called. Some—other people—may not be cognizant of this. Along the way, God **may** also raise up "destiny facilitators" that will have been chosen to work in coordination with you, or for your benefit. You will NOT have to seek them out. They will arrive at the right time ... and in the Grand Design.

Now, if you add to your patience PRINCIPLES OF VALUE and GODLINESS, you will have the spiritual and physical mechanics to add other people, like-minded associates, to your asset bank for success and continued vision.

▣ PRINCIPLES OF VALUE PLUS GODLINESS

One of the great aspects of reading and studying---as well as meditating upon---the Holy Bible daily is so we can learn precepts and principles. We can learn HOW God thinks about certain things and WHY He wants us to behave in a particular manner. **Situations vary in life; we may not always come up against situations that have been codified**. However, if we know HOW God thinks about certain things and WHY God expects certain responses from us, then we can **transfer those principles** into every arena of life.

➡ Ask God to give you discernment over:

- **People**
- **Things**
- **Situations**

We need to know both the Old Testament (Tanakh) and the New Testament (Brit Chadashah) so we can navigate successfully through the issues of life and have continued vision. **There is an association between the Law of God and the Vision from Him!**

"The law is no more; her prophets also find no vision from the Lord." [Lamentations 2:9]

"Where there is no vision, the people perish: but he that keeps the law, happy is he." [Proverbs 29:18]

It is the same way in our personal lives and ministries. If we adhere to the teachings of God; that is, live by the principles we learn about HOW God thinks and WHY He expects certain behavior, then we will not only have SUCCESS but also continued VISION.

Actually the combined traits of PRINCIPLES OF VALUE and GODLINESS will be concomitant factors. Here again is the key: knowing and obeying the Word of God, which is His Will.

☐ LIKE-MINDED ASSOCIATES PLUS BROTHERLY KINDNESS

You need to have strong relationships with God and with those people to whom God will lead you to work. Appreciate the people with which God has chosen you to work. However, don't try to "force" relationships: don't make commitments to every person you meet. God will show you those people to whom you should be committed when you are FIRST committed to Him!

Give positive support, or "reinforcement" to those people you're committed to ...

> ☞ Whether they are OVER YOU in a position of authority;

> ☞ You are OVER THEM; or,

> ☞ You are on the same level (working or collaborative associates).

Remind each other that *"God will fight for us!"* Give your associates REWARDS from time-to-time for:

> ☞ The good work they do;

> ☞ Their consistency and faithfulness; or,

> ☞ Their availability.

These rewards do not (always) have to be monetary. Sometimes a "pat on the back" or a "word of encouragement" is really meaningful: letting them know the good they are doing is not going unnoticed. Let people **know** that you are **thankful** and are **appreciative** of their association with you.

Maybe you can schedule an invitation to dinner, or just spending time alone with them or their family, whether it's a few minutes or a day or two. It is also important for a man to give positive support to his wife. There are so many ways a wife serves a husband in his professional life that **may** go unnoticed by him. The opposite is true, also, for a professional wife.

We need to appreciate those nearest to us, and never to take them for granted. **This is where "family altar" is so important: don't neglect ministering to your own family!** They may be the GREATEST SUCCESS. Read and discuss the Holy Bible together, and then pray together.

It is good to spend time refreshing your mind thinking about all the successes God has given you in the past. God has NOT brought you this far to make you fail. God is FOR you! One time the disciples of Jesus were in a ship in the middle of the sea where the waves were rough and the wind was strong. They became fearful until Jesus came to them on the water and told them not to be afraid. They FORGOT that the Lord had commanded them to GO to the other side.

He did NOT intend them to sink or to fail. **Jesus intends for you to SUCCEED!** Take time to study in the Holy Bible how others have succeeded: Abraham, Joseph, Daniel, Esther, Mordecai, Deborah ... Paul.

Associate with like-minded people who SHARE YOUR VISION (or who know what you're about) . . . people who are POSITIVE. You want to be able to brainstorm with these people, and not to have ideas-- no matter how ridiculous--be shot down as soon as they are verbalized.

IMPORTANT

This group of like-minded people with whom you will share your vision, goals, and new ideas, is NOT an accountability group. This is NOT a group of people to whom you decide to be accountable for your personal life, your profession or your finances. This is a group of people with whom you need to have OPENNESS for CREATIVITY:

- To dream;

- To plan;

- To get feedback; and,

- To implement.

We have seen that when we add to our patience the twin gift of *Principles of Value PLUS Godliness*, we will have the spiritual and physical mechanics to add other people, *Like-minded Associates*, to our asset bank for success cycles and continued--*organic*--vision. Next, you will want to be prepared for selecting your *Vehicle for Attainment*.

◻ VEHICLE FOR ATTAINMENT PLUS LOVE

What is the means by which you will arrive at your goal? What is the vehicle which will transport you to the attainment of your dream?

When an athlete in a championship game scores the winning goal, he is merely manifesting a composite of the years of training, wins and losses, experience, exercise, and mental conditioning that have preceded this moment. Likewise, the composite of major decisions in our lives are usually the summation of the smaller minor decisions and habit-patterns we have formed along the way.

To some people, the vehicle for attainment of their goals is a multilevel marketing plan. To others, it is a business and investment plan. To many, it is a retirement plan. To the **ultimate winner**, it is **the vision and the miraculous arrived at through seeking God in prayer and fasting**: combining *Enthusiastic Desire PLUS Faith* with DIRECTION from God.

God will reveal YOUR vehicle for attainment as you spend time alone with Him. Shut off your television and your video / DVD player ... spend time with the Creator of the Universe. Talk to Him and listen to Him. God is NOT stupid. **The Heavenly Father knows the**

person who wants to be used by Him: the person who wants to spend time with Him.

The Creator will reveal by His Spirit the vehicle for you to use in the attainment of your goals---and when to **change** that vehicle. God, the creator of the desires in your heart, knows the methodology by which to bring them to pass. **He knows the vehicle by which, when coupled with FAITH, will bring the goal-desires into fruition.**

There is an amazing spiritual truth we find in Torah in Genesis 11:1-9. Before the nations of the earth were scattered on the face of the earth, the earth was of one language and one speech. The people had decided to make a city and a tower, the top of which would reach unto heaven. They wanted to make a name for themselves so they would not be scattered abroad upon the face of the earth.

"And the Lord said, 'Behold, the people is one, and they all have one language; and this they begin to do: and now nothing will be restrained from them, which they have imagined to do." [verse 6]

"Let us go down, and there confound their language, that they may not understand one another's speech." [verse 7]

Archaeological records show us that these were wicked and idolatrous people. Yet we see in verse 6 that God said, "nothing will be restrained from them." Notice they had ONE goal and ONE speech. **They were unified in purpose and language**.

If this principle of "oneness" works in unbelievers ... for ungodly, wicked people ... how much more will it work for believers--for God's people--who have ONE goal and ONE speech: **a common vision and a common language**. Especially Spirit-filled Christians who have a common objective and **who can pray and decree a thing** (or a set of objectives) in not only **their common earthly language, but also their heavenly language: tongues!**

In Job 22:28 we read, *"You shall also decree a thing, and it shall be established unto you ..."* In the original Hebrew language the word "decree" is a primitive root form of the word **"gazar,"** which means **"to cut out exclusively, or to decide."** In its primitive form it is used also as a "quarrying" term ... as in cutting out stone from a rock quarry.

It means more than to "say" or "speak." **It conveys the meaning of "cutting something out in your mind's eye."** That is, "to envision [to make a vision], to decide upon it, and confess it" ... and then it will be established unto you. If you and your fellow believers in fait—or your associates--have a common vision or goal, and decide upon it, confessing it in a common language, speaking it ... *"nothing will be restrained from you which you have imagined (or, envisioned) to do!!* [Read again Genesis 11:1-6.]

▶ **The SECRET**: The capstone to the whole process--without which you will not be the ULTIMATE WINNER--is **LOVE**.

No matter how intense your desire, the vehicle for attainment of your goals, your faith and the other twins

41

we have studied, cannot bring you into success and continued vision without LOVE. Love is the channel through which the gifts of the Holy Spirit work. *"Faith works by love."* [Galatians 5:6]

➡ If you feel that you are lacking in love, then pray and ask God to give you His love for people. It works.

Remember … if you have LOVE, faith can work!

It is a wonderful thing to have FAITH, but if you have a PLAN incorporating your desires to go along with your faith, it is even better! Here's a SECRET that will allow you to SEE many MIRACLES:

If your PLAN fits into God's plan …

You will have God's FAITH … and

God's faith ALWAYS WORKS!

It is anointed with LOVE!

I trust this book, **Success Cycles and Secrets**, has been a blessing to you, and that it will help you accomplish your God-given desires **continuously**.

LIVE A LIFE OF EXCELLENCE!

After you read **Success Cycles and Secrets**, you will want to study two other companion books in the **Success Series** by Prince Handley:

Action Keys for Success

How to Do Great Works

UNIVERSITY OF EXCELLENCE PRESS
Los Angeles ▪ London ▪ Tel Aviv

OTHER BOOKS BY PRINCE HANDLEY

- Map of the End Times

- How to Do Great Works

- Flow Chart of Revelation

- Action Keys for Success

- Health and Healing Complete Guide to Wholeness

- Prophetic Calendar for Israel and the Nations (2014-2023)

- Healing Deliverance

- How to Receive God's Power with Gifts of the Spirit

- Healing for Mental and Physical Abuse

- Victory Over Opposition and Resistance

- Healing of Emotional Wounds

- How to Be Healed and Live in Divine Health

- Healing from Fear, Shame and Anger

- How to Receive Healing and Bring Healing to Others

- New Global Strategy: Enabling Missions

- The Art of Christian Warfare

AVAILABLE AT AMAZON AND OTHER BOOK STORES
UNIVERSITY OF EXCELLENCE PRESS